How to Stop
STUTTERING

FOR ANYONE

A Self-Therapy Approach to Conquering Stubborn Stutters,
Regaining Your Voice, and Leading a Fulfilled Life

Jesse Craven

To All Stutterers

To all the brave souls who battle morning to night, enduring the anguish of a silenced voice, this dedication is woven with boundless admiration and fervent hope. In the tapestry of life's challenges, the intricate threads of stuttering have crafted a unique path, we celebrate your unwavering strength, perseverance, and unwritten triumphs.

To the nights spent wrestling with self-doubt and the mornings of battles fought within; your courage is a testament to the indomitable human spirit. Your journey, though marred with challenges, has sculpted you into a warrior who refuses to be silenced, crafting a self-portrait of resilience, tenacity, and unwavering determination.

To the sleepless nights spent rehearsing conversations, the moments of desperation when words failed to synchronize with thoughts, and the countless instances your voice was reduced to a mere whisper, know that we see you, we hear you, and we believe in you.

May this book serve as a sanctuary, a safe haven where you can discover life-altering strategies, a roadmap towards conquering your stutter and unlocking the limitless potential that resides within you. With every turn of the page, we aim to embolden you, to fill your spirit with the conviction that you are not alone.

Contents

Preface

Stuttering, also known as stammering, is a relentless adversary that affects millions of people around the world. Its debilitating grasp can engulf even the most confident individuals, causing communication to be a daily struggle. The anxiety, frustration, and isolation that stuttering inflicts can be overwhelming, leaving one feeling invisible in a world that eagerly awaits their voice. But it doesn't have to be this way.

In the pages that follow, I will share with you a deeply personal and honest approach to my journey to fluency. I offer you my experiences, my failures, and ultimately, my success in overcoming the formidable chains of stuttering. This book is not a panacea, nor is it a magical cure. Rather, it is a guide born out of my own self-taught therapy and countless hours of introspection.

Allow me to acquaint you with my story—a story that unveils the hidden intricacies of the stuttering mind and the techniques that can pave the way to fluency. Like many others who walk this path, mine began long ago, in the moments where words were held captive within my stuttering lips. As a teenager, I felt the unrelenting weight of speech impediment on my shoulders—a weight that grew heavier with each passing day.

The anguish and frustration I experienced during those formative years are difficult to express. The simplest of conversations became battlegrounds of vulnerability, where each word struggled to break free from the confines of my stuttering tongue. I held my breath, afraid to let my voice be heard, afraid of the judgment that awaited me.

Yet, amidst the struggle, a fire ignited within me—a burning determination to conquer the chains that bound me. I began to immerse myself in the world of self-therapy, exploring various techniques, experimenting with different approaches, and analyzing the psychological aspects that intertwined with my stuttering. The techniques I discovered were not flashy or miraculous, but they were the building blocks of my transformation.

Through unwavering determination and a willingness to confront my deepest insecurities, I slowly unlocked the door to my voice. Each small victory became a stepping stone towards a future free from the burden of stuttering. Gradually, the shackles of my stutter fell away, liberating me to embrace the world with newfound fluency.

The techniques and exercises that I have developed over the years are not revolutionary concepts, but rather a combination of tried and tested methods that worked for me. They are the culmination of my own experience and the wisdom I gained from countless hours of self-reflection and research. In this book, I offer them to you, not as a one-size-fits-all solution, but as tools to be adapted and personalized to fit your journey towards fluency.

I implore you to approach this book with an open mind and a willingness to challenge yourself. Stuttering is a deeply ingrained habit—one that requires patience, persistence, and self-compassion to overcome. It is my hope that by sharing the lessons I have learned and the techniques I have honed, you will find solace and guidance in your own healing journey.

Remember, this book is a testament to the power of self-therapy and self-discovery. It is a beacon of hope for those who yearn to unshackle their voices and find freedom from the constraints of stuttering. Together, we can navigate the treacherous waters of speech impediment and emerge on the shores of fluency and confidence.

Let us embark on this transformative journey together, hand in hand, as we navigate the terrain of stuttering and discover the beauty and strength that lies within. May this book be a guiding light on your path to triumph over stuttering and finding your authentic voice.

1

The Therapy Approach

This book, which is written in the second person to explain what you can and should do to control your stuttering, is written to and for the large population of adults and teenagers that stutter. We can say with confidence that if you stutter, you don't have to give in to your speech impediment helplessly since you can alter the way you speak. You can develop your communication skills such that it comes naturally to you. While there is no quick fix for stuttering, self-therapy can be successful with the appropriate approach.

You might be wary of any strategy that claims that it will provide a solution because of past experience. It's possible that you've attempted various therapeutic approaches in the past and were let down or disillusioned by them. This book makes no deceptive claims or quick-fix magical cure promises. It explains what you can and should do to boost your confidence and get through the challenge.

It provides a rationale, realistic treatment plan based on techniques and processes that have been proven effective in speech clinics and other academic settings. It has been demonstrated that this therapy strategy is effective.

We begin by making two presumptions. One is that you don't have any physical flaws or speech-related impairments that would prevent you from speaking more fluently. After all, when you're by yourself or unaware of other people's listening or watching, you probably don't stutter when speaking. Almost everyone who stutters occasionally speaks fluently, and the majority do so occasionally.

We also presume that you might not be able to hire a speech pathologist who is qualified to work with you to solve your problem in the way that is outlined in this book and that you will therefore need to be your therapist. Authorities concur that stuttering therapy is essentially a do-it-yourself job even with qualified instruction.

You must have a strong drive to overcome your obstacle and a serious commitment to completing the recommended processes and assignments if you are genuinely interested in improving your speech. The only person on the planet who can help you with your stuttering is you.

It is impossible to overstate the significance of motivation, and whether or not therapy is successful depends on your willingness to stick with it. It won't be simple, but it is possible. However, despite what you may have read, there is no way to guarantee success in this program or any other because there is currently no proven 'cure' for stuttering.

But it is conceivable that if you implement the advice and follow the steps indicated in this book, you will be able to manage your stuttering and talk normally without any abnormalities. You can overcome your stuttering if others have. However, the best method for you to determine whether a therapy is helpful is to give it a try and let the outcomes speak for themselves.

It should be noted that stutterers differ greatly from one another. The frequency and intensity of stuttering often vary from time to time and from one scenario to another. Some cases are moderate, while others are severe. Sometimes you may be able to talk rather fluently with little to no difficulty; other times you may experience significant difficulties, especially when the message that needs to be communicated is vital. This makes it a particularly frustrating disorder because it can and frequently does get worse in particular settings and situations.

The majority of stutterers seem to struggle the most when they're ashamed or worried about something. One guy put it this way: *"If you can't afford to stutter, you will."*

It might be more obvious when requested to state your name, while speaking to people in positions of authority like potential employers or teachers, when making introductions, when addressing groups, when talking on the phone, etc. Conversely, you can struggle less or not at all when speaking to a youngster, a pet animal, or yourself.

It should be noted that stutterers differ greatly in their responses, personality traits, and the circumstances in which they stutter. Since each stutterer has established their unique pattern of stuttering, no two people stutter in the same way. Your responses may differ from others because people who stutter all have a wide range of personality qualities. As a result, we kindly ask you to be patient when reading about problems that you may not personally experience but which may be problematic for others.

Most people possess some abilities that are a little surprising. The majority of people who stutter typically have little to no trouble whether they sing, shout, whisper, or read aloud together with others.

You can tell if you have the physical capacity to speak normally if you don't have any trouble speaking when you're among other people, reading, or speaking aloud. It would be evident if you were physically able to speak normally but fear may force you to put unneeded strain into your speech mechanism, which could cause the majority of your difficulty.

In this regard, it should be noted that the average stutterer's I.Q. (intellectual quotient) is thought to be normal or above average, so this in no way implies that there is a mental disability present.

The Root Causes of Your Stuttering

Many stutterers have had the false impression that if the "cause" could only be identified, a quick recovery would follow. Numerous hypotheses regarding the nature and causes of stuttering have been put forth, however, none of them have been supported as of yet.

A lot of study is being done to look at any potential neurological connection, hemispheric dominance, and other potential causes of a lack of coordination between the speech muscles that lead to stuttering. Some stutterers are also affected by hereditary causes.

Whatever the source or causes, you should focus on what you are doing right now that prolongs your difficulty rather than what happened in the past. You don't need to continue stuttering helplessly for the rest of your life. You can develop self-assurance in your capacity for open communication. You too can succeed, as others have done.

2

The Influential Factors in Stuttering Therapy

A few pertinent issues should be raised before going over the precise therapeutic procedures. This is so that they can alter how you feel about and what you think about treatment, as well as how you can and should work on it. These variables contain information on topics that can significantly affect therapy progress, variables such as;

o Feelings and emotions
o Distractions
o Tension and relaxation
o Getting other people's support
o Determination

We'll start by highlighting how feelings and emotions can—and frequently do—affect how serious your problem is.

Feelings and Emotions

Stuttering is a very complex speech impediment,It is a disorder with both physical and emotional components. The latter can be demonstrated by the claim that stuttering is mostly what the stutterer does when trying to avoid stuttering. Stuttering is, in other words, similar to a brilliant prank you pull on yourself. You're more likely to stammer as you tighten up in response to your stuttering and your sentiments over stuttering.

What occurs is that you try to force trouble-free speech because you want to quit stuttering so desperately. Additionally, when you use greater energy, your speaking mechanism becomes more tense and you are more likely to experience problems. The delicate balance of the speech system means that the more you consciously try to stop stuttering, the worse it unintentionally gets.

Since stuttering might be difficult, it has an emotional impact. Even if it's not true, you can even believe that stuttering is a shame. You might now be quite sensitive about your problem as a result. It is true that being blocked or unable to express yourself verbally without stuttering can be extremely irritating. As a result, in certain cases, you could feel so humiliated and embarrassed that you experience feelings of hopelessness, inadequacy, sadness, and perhaps self-hatred.

Your emotions may cause you to feel so fearful and anxious that it affects how you interact with other people and how you view the world in general. Your personality can change as a result of stuttering, you may start to change the way you speak and development will happen more quickly if you can desensitize yourself and realize that you don't need to panic when you stammer or anticipate stuttering.

Positive adjustments to your thoughts and feelings regarding your stuttering and yourself will result in positive adjustments to your speech. Stuttering phobias can be associated with specific words, noises, people, situations, the telephone, saying your name, job interviews, etc. When you don't feel as anxious, you're generally not going to struggle as much.

When your fear is intense, it causes your speech mechanism to become tense, which causes you to stutter more frequently and forcefully. This fear can occasionally be so intense that it makes you agitated and nearly renders you incapable of thinking or acting.

You might be prevented from engaging in events and experiences that you would otherwise find enjoyable by such fear or anxiety. The more embarrassed and ashamed you feel as a result of this, the more probable it is that you will stammer.

One guy always put it this way: *"If you can't afford to stutter, you will."* As a result, the degree of fear you experience usually in proportion with how much you stutter

Distractions

You probably wouldn't have any issues if you could find a technique to divert your attention from feelings of dread and away from your stutter. We don't know how you could acquire such a *"forgettery,"* but if you could, you might be able to stop stuttering altogether.

Generally, anything that takes your thoughts off of your worry or the possibility of stuttering can provide you with some temporary comfort. This is the major reason why complex techniques like speaking with a sing-song accent, using a metronome, speaking while tapping a finger, swinging an arm, or stamping a foot, etc., can occasionally fool stutterers. These and numerous more peculiar speech patterns could lead to momentary fluency.

Even just considering how to employ them when difficulty is imminent diverts your focus from stuttering. They might momentarily block off fearful thoughts, but neither fear nor stuttering will be permanently reduced. As strange as it may seem, any stutterer who has faith in a new or strange technique will benefit from it for a while—at least until the novelty wears off.

Tension and Relaxation

Since fear causes excessive muscle tension, therapy should focus on reducing it. Fear-induced tension plays a crucial role in activating your stuttering and may be the immediate source of your problem. You wouldn't stutter as frequently, or at the very least, you wouldn't stammer as readily, if you didn't try to force trouble-free speech.

Though it is challenging to respond to how anxiety can be lessened, hypnotism has been proposed as a potential solution. It would be nice if you could obtain some kind of hypnotic treatment to ease your stress, but hypnosis has not been proven to have any long-lasting effects.

Many stutterers have experimented with drinking alcohol or being mildly intoxicated in an effort to unwind. For some people, this could cause stuttering changes, but this is only a transient impact. It cannot, of course, be advised.

Unfortunately, there are currently no medications that have been authorized particularly for stuttering, despite new medications that reduce anxiety and panic being available. Furthermore, medications frequently come with a unique set of adverse effects that add to the issue.

Additionally, it has been asserted that practicing relaxation techniques will help you get rid of or at least lessen the tension you feel. It would be beneficial if you could develop relaxation techniques that would ease tension and remain effective when you stutter.

Many people who stammer have invested many hours trying out these techniques in the hope that they may be effective in their time of need. This topic has been the subject of extensive research. The outcomes, however, have not been satisfying.

Even though learning to relax is not suggested as a solution to the issue, it can always be beneficial to your speech, overall health, and well-being. The underlying tenet is that stuttering will decrease as your level of calmness and relaxation increases. One reason for this is that it will encourage a calmer and more relaxed way of speaking, therefore you will be asked to speak in a smooth, leisurely, easy, and deliberate manner.

Specific muscle relaxation is more useful than overall relaxation. You can learn to relax those muscles during speech if you can identify the area that is the most tense. Only a few muscles, including those that govern your lips, tongue, mouth, breath, and to some extent your vocal cords, are used in these workouts. You can practice purposefully tensing and then relaxing those muscles when you're calm and alone. It will be beneficial if you can let these muscles down when speaking.

Additionally advised is the daily practice of bodily exercises. Physical activity is believed to be beneficial for one's health as well as for fostering the self-confidence that all stutterers require. Exercises for the body can encourage a tendency to stand up straight, with the head held high and the shoulders back. This type of forceful stance can aid in creating a sense of self-confidence, or the conviction that you are at least as excellent as the next person. You will benefit from physical activity in this regard.

Try to have a generally upbeat mood. Remind yourself that you can and will get through your challenge. You will advance more quickly if you adopt an assertive mindset and pair it with regulated approaches. Be confident and forceful, and have faith in your abilities.

Getting Other People's Support

It would be nice if you could get in touch with a qualified speech-language pathologist who specializes in stuttering for assistance. This self-therapy program, however, has been designed with the possibility that you may not have such specialist assistance in mind. Even if you succeed, your efforts will still play a significant role in the success of any program.

This does not imply that you should reject assistance from others because you will need individuals to converse and practice. A family member or close friend that you have a strong and trustworthy relationship with may be able to provide you with useful assistance in a variety of ways.

Such a person might be able to see and hear things that you would not be aware of when acting as an observer. Such a friend might mimic your stuttering to help you become conscious of what you are doing when you are having difficulty while you are studying the way you stutter. Or, he or she may go along with you on some of your assignments, give you praise for your efforts, and offer you moral support by motivating you to keep going and keep trying until you succeed. You will require all the inspiration you can muster.

Sometimes well-meaning friends will give you unsolicited advice on how to stop stuttering based on what they have heard or what they believe you should do. Even if such counsel may be unwise and unwelcome, we contend that it should be graciously embraced despite being based on a poor grasp of the issue.

Stutterers' support groups have been established in various locations. They get together frequently to support one another in solving their problems. Such a group may be very beneficial if its leaders are competent.

Determination

Fluency does not come easily. Therapy needs to be persistent in order to be effective. You must have the guts to face your stuttering head-on and take on assignments that will be difficult and likely cause you a lot of shame. Does speaking more fluently merit the work required to generate it? That is totally up to you.

Actually, your shame will assist lessen the sensitivity that exacerbates your stuttering. It will also be simpler for you to maintain the required level of presence of mind to follow through on the suggested measures as you become less sensitive to your difficulties. If you consider your stuttering to be a disability, you should look for solutions to improve your life through more fluent speech. You must feel more positive about who you are as a person.

You wish to talk more openly, but you shouldn't demand or expect perfection. To accomplish this, you must have the willpower to alter both your personality and the way you speak. You may regain control and become a master of your speech with the help of these improvements.

We assert that you can succeed and that the benefits outweigh the costs. Though to shift your perspective on your issue will require a commitment on your behalf. The disability of stuttering is tenacious and will not readily give up. Therapy is difficult. Your choice is up to you.

3

Establishing the Premise and Program for Effective Therapy Procedures

The notion that stuttering is a behavior that may be altered or changed is the foundation for the concepts presented in this book. This indicates that you can learn to regulate your difficulties, in part by altering your thoughts and feelings around stuttering, and in part by getting rid of or fixing the irregular behaviors that are connected to your stuttering.

In order to do this, you will need to discipline yourself to face your concerns and stop being as sensitive about your stuttering. And it will consist of three steps.

☐Examining your stuttering behavior
☐Cutting out any superfluous or unusual behavior
☐Taking actions to reduce your blocks

The fundamental idea is that stuttering is something you do and that you can learn to stop doing it.

We briefly explain how this program operates because you must comprehend the whole therapy strategy. You will be required to try out a useful therapy technique that is outlined later in this chapter. For individuals who feel they require urgent relief, this will be especially helpful. Then, it is advised that you go by twelve sensible advice or ground principles to enhance your speech. These guidelines are meant to give you effective strategies for handling your situation.

You will be focusing on lessening the intensity and abnormality of your trouble as well as the number of your stutterings by adhering to the suggestions of these beneficial ground rules. Additionally, by following these instructions, you will gradually establish the foundation for regaining positive control over your speech.

These guidelines will nudge you to:
• Speak more thoughtfully
• Stutter easily and openly
• Not trying to hide your stuttering
• Avoid all avoidance techniques

• Halt all secondary symptoms
• Keep normal eye contact

You will need to conduct a thorough analysis of what your speech mechanism is doing incorrectly when you stammer. Find out just what you are doing when you are having difficulty. With the help of this crucial information, you will be able to alter the behaviors that are causing your speech problems and learn better stuttering management techniques.

Instead of viewing your stuttering as a flaw or as something that just happens to you, you should think of it as something you have learned to do. You should endeavor to replace the unfavorable methods of responding that you have learned with the regular speaking behavior that you are fundamentally capable of.

Next, you will be shown how to remedy these errors utilizing post-block, in-block, and pre-block techniques. These are the technical titles of the techniques you will learn to enable you to move effortlessly through fearful phrases in a planned way and give you a sense of control.

You will have made strides in your ability to manage your voice once you can follow the rules. Because they may hit your weak places, some rules may have a greater impact on your stuttering and signify more to you than others. As a result, you'll discover that following some principles to their fulfillment will advance your situation more than others.

We are unable to determine the specific manner in which you stutter, therefore we can only advise that you make an effort to adhere to all of the suggestions.

Depending on the seriousness of your case and how determined you are to complete the assignments, the time required to complete each rule's aim will vary greatly. It's possible that the amount of time needed to accomplish a goal can be expressed in days. Others, on the other hand, might take a long period to break some obstinate or seemingly intractable habits.

You are recommended to complete each stage of the program, even if your stuttering is only slight. Additionally, as you complete a guideline, we hope you will feel certain that you have successfully accomplished its objective before moving on to the next one. You will be fully aware of your situation and your development if you do this.

Every stutterer should strive to learn self-help skills. The first thing you should do is experiment with a different speaking style, as explained in the next outline. This is made to provide you with some relief right away.

Beneficial Therapeutic Technique

This procedure is especially for stutterers who feel like they need some sort of temporary relief right now. However, since it can improve your speaking fluency, it is advised that you give this experimental technique a try.

It entails speaking for a lengthy period of time extremely slowly and smoothly. When speaking slowly, it is advised to give each word or syllable's beginning or starting sound at least a second to slide through. Then, keep extending words, syllables, and sounds in a fluent, easy-onset way.

This easy and slow drawn-out way of speaking, especially in the first words, can't help but relieve you. Those who do not have many strong negative thoughts regarding their stuttering may find it to be especially beneficial.

We advise you to try this method. You might not initially enjoy the sound or sensation, but keep in mind that changing anything almost always causes discomfort. As a result, we advise against using this approach exclusively at first. Allow yourself some time to get used to this new way of communicating.

You are aware that sounds make up words. You are instructed to begin the sounds of your words in this technique by gently and effortlessly sliding through the first sound at an exceedingly slow, easy, smooth rate. This could entail pausing for as long as a second or more between the sounds that begin your words. We refer to this as "easy onset."

Next, use continuous phonation to extend and lengthen all sounds as you vocalize them. Almost all consonant and vowel sounds must be lengthened and prolonged, and the transition from one sound to the next must be slowed down.

Start your vocal cords vibrating softly, steadily, and very slowly while you start to speak in this easy onset style with light pressure on your tongue and lips, also known as "light contacts." Placing your palm on your throat, where the vibrations should be felt, can allow you to determine whether your vocal cords are vibrating.

You will have continuity of sound and airflow with no interruption in your voicing and no repetitions if you start and prolong all sounds in this incredibly slow, drawn-out manner. To repeat, extend and prolong each sound you voice, especially the starting sounds. And make gentle, effortless contacts on the consonants to extend all transitions between all sounds (vowel and consonant).

Vowel sounds are simple to lengthen and prolong, but many of the consonant sounds require practice. Spend some time alone learning how to prolong consonant sounds because some of them, like b, p, d, t, etc., are plosive and must be pronounced gently and slowly with loose tongue and mouth contacts.

Both feared and unfeared phrases should be spoken in this fluent, leisurely, easy-onset, drawn-out style. In other words, until you get the hang of it, you should do it every time you speak. Connect the sounds of your words by tying the first letter of one word to the last letter of the one before it.

Even if speaking at this slow, calm pace of only 30 words per minute may make you feel awkward or ashamed, you must explore its benefits. Again, it is advised that you employ this slow, lengthy method of speech when conversing with people only after you have practiced it extensively alone.

You could be reluctant to speak in this manner because you believe people will question your motives. Inform them that you are working to improve your stuttering. Nothing to be embarrassed about, and your buddies will be happy to assist. If no problems arise after utilizing this way of speaking for a while, one may progressively raise the rate at which the words are started and uttered. In this situation, you should return to the slower pace at which you were comfortable.

This method of talking slowly and naturally, which is frequently utilized, can be quite relieving and make it easier for you to speak. Even if it might not be a perfect solution, it will almost certainly be beneficial.

In any case, it will demonstrate to you and others that you view your stuttering as a challenge rather than a curse and are making an effort to deal with it. People value that outlook. Start right away.

Work diligently on the program as outlined above for a while—possibly a couple of weeks or longer. When that time comes, you'll be aware of the advantages of this therapy approach.

4

The Vital Ground Rules for Successful Therapy

We hope that practicing the method recommended in the previous chapter made it easier for you to communicate. However, for several reasons, we do not advise that you use this style of speaking consistently. First off, it might not always or in all circumstances work for you. When you're anxious or thrilled, it could be challenging to remember to employ the fluency shaping approaches. Second, you might not feel at ease using this tone of voice with all of your listeners.

The guidelines in this chapter show how to control your stuttering by putting some fundamental remedial techniques into practice. These are made up of twelve crucial rules that succinctly describe this program. They provide a rough description of how you can utilize two strategies to manage your issue.

Firstly, by reducing your speech phobias and avoidance behaviors, you might start by changing your thoughts and attitudes regarding your stuttering.

Second, by changing the abnormal behaviors linked to your stuttering through the use of specific strategies that will alter the form of your stuttering and allow you to speak normally.

There are twelve ground rules to be followed, stuttering is a challenging disorder, thus we are unable to provide a less sophisticated therapy. Therefore, it is recommended to utilize all of the accessible strategies that might contribute to the resolution of your situation.

It is advised that you first thoroughly read through and learn the regulations that are outlined on the pages that follow. You must try your hardest to abide by each of these in order to improve, focusing on one at a time. Although it is up to you, it is recommended to deal with them in the order that they are listed. As stated, the principles are intended to stop any avoidance behaviors and first help you become less sensitive about your stuttering. After that, you'll focus on fixing what you're doing incorrectly when you stammer.

An important rule will require you to conduct a thorough analysis of the strange things your speech mechanism is performing when you stammer to achieve the latter goal. Following that, you will be able to stop performing the things that are unnecessary for you to do so and make the necessary corrections.

You will be given instructions on how to repair your improper speech mechanism behaviors using post-block, in-block, and pre-block remedies. These phrases refer to techniques made to make it easier for you to flow through dreaded words in a planned way so you may feel in charge. It won't be simple to work toward achieving the goals of these regulations; in fact, it might be a tedious, worrisome process. It will need effort and time to alter your speaking pattern in addition to your efforts to reduce your fear of difficulty.

Because they target your weak points, some rules may have a greater impact on you than others and help you stutter less. As a result, you might discover that following some rules will advance you further than following others. We are unable to identify your specific areas of weakness, so all we can advise is that you adhere to all of the recommendations. Keep in mind that you are your own therapist, and if you break any of these guidelines, you might not have someone to watch over you. While outcomes are what you need and want, perfect compliance is neither feasible nor expected.

Your improvement should depend on focusing on these helpful techniques and modifying your stutter. It can be preferable to focus on making an effort to abide by only one guideline at a time. Even though it could take a while, when you believe you have completed the task with the required results, move on to the next rule.

Plan your practice sessions around daily routines like mealtimes, lunch breaks, and getting to and from work or school. In general, unplanned practice results in little to no practice.

Make an honest attempt to follow each of these rules as closely as you are able. It will be beneficial. Have faith in your abilities to move on and give yourself a powerful dose of willpower. The steps to take in order to work toward reaching each rule's goal will be clearly described in the chapters that follow.

(Some people with stuttering experience little to no shame and embarrassment about it. They should not worry as much as

other people do about the regulations designed to lessen shame and embarrassment.)

Here they are—let's go!

1. Whether you stammer or not, develop the practice of speaking slowly and deliberately at all times.

Going too slowly is preferable to going too quickly. Slow down because it is simpler to control a sluggish turtle than a quick bunny. The first rule instructs you to develop the practice of speaking slowly and deliberately at all times. This encourages a speech pattern that is widely respected. However, the main reason it is advised is that it will provide a more diversified and laid-back speaking style that is more receptive to therapeutic techniques.

Additionally, speaking slowly tends to lessen any sense of urgency that stutterers may occasionally experience when asked to speak. Some people speak too quickly to finish their sentences before they stutter or block. This only serves to increase tension and make their stuttering worse.

It is also advised to frequently pause briefly between phrases (or words) when speaking to help with time management. This will decrease the effects of time pressure.

Accepting your stuttering for the time being, commit to always speaking slowly and thoughtfully. It could be difficult and need concentration, especially if you have a habit of speaking quickly. At first, it could seem awkward as well, but if you can get used to this way of speaking, it will help. The biggest benefit is that you will have significantly less time pressure.

2. Avoid talking forcefully but prolong the initial sounds of the words you are afraid to say when you begin to speak.

This entails speaking strongly while allowing your voice to flow naturally into word sounds and using light, loose movements of your lips, tongue, and jaw. The most crucial piece of advice is slipping into the words as easily and calmly as you can when you stutter. Your intensity and frequency of stuttering will decrease if you can follow this one rule and allow yourself to stutter naturally.

This rule also suggests that you lengthen the first sound of any word you are afraid of when speaking easily. Additionally, you should emphasize drawing out the transition to the subsequent sound or sounds in the word. Only the phrases you fear are meant by this.

Here, it is not advised that you amplify each word's sound. Some people attempt to deal with their issues by pulling their lips together, forcing their tongue firmly against their lips, or pressing their tongue firmly against the roof of their mouth while simultaneously closing up their airways. This is illogical. A corked bottle won't allow you to pour water from it. Find out how easily you stammer.

Replace your strange and annoying habits with simpler stuttering techniques. stutter quietly and with ease. You'll notice the distinction.

3. Stutter out loud; do not attempt to conceal your stuttering.

Bring it up in the open; there is no benefit to acting like a typical speaker. Stuttering simply becomes worse when you try to disguise it. Inform others you speak with about your stuttering, and adopt a stance of being willing to stammer freely. Your guilt and embarrassment over your situation will be lessened if you adopt an honest attitude.

Your dread of difficulty only tends to grow when you feel guilty or embarrassed. Additionally, the worry of difficulty contributes to the tightening or tension of your speaking muscles, which makes your issue worse. Most stutterers would be less sensitive about their issues and experience considerably less trouble if they did not try to disguise the fact that they stutter. Desensitizing yourself and boosting your confidence are challenging tasks since it takes time to overcome fear. But the more you put effort into it, the happier you'll be.

Use the methods you have learned to freely practice to lessen the frequency and severity of your stuttering blocks. This should make it easier for you to use them. So let's attempt to eliminate any anxiety you may have about your speaking by voluntarily telling others you stammer. Find opportunities to talk about it with the people you interact with. Inform them that you are honing your speech.

This important rule is to increase your capacity for stress tolerance and boost your self-assurance through desensitization.

You will be encouraged to occasionally stutter on purpose as part of this rule. You might be able to relieve the anxiety and worry that worsen your issue by purposefully doing what you fear.

4. Recognize and get rid of any odd body motions, facial tics, or gestures you could make when stuttering or trying to avoid difficulty.

This has nothing to do with the improper use of your vocal muscles, which will be carefully examined later. The aforementioned rule applies to needless movements or mannerisms that may characterize your specific stuttering pattern; they are referred to as *"secondary symptoms."*

Head jerks, eye blinking or closing, hand or arm twitching, ear pulling, knee-slapping, raised eyebrows, grimaces, finger tapping, hand covering lips, etc. are examples of secondary symptoms. Discovering and identifying any secondary symptoms you may have will be required to achieve this. You must have this knowledge to take action to get rid of them. These are terrible habits that you may have picked up thinking would make it easier for you to talk, but they instead make your stuttering more weird.

It's possible that you don't exhibit any such unusual actions, but thoroughly examine yourself as instructed in the chapter on removing secondary symptoms. If you discover that you engage in these behaviors, let's try to eliminate them. They are not required for speech production.

5. Try your best to break any habits of avoidance, postponement, or substitution that you may have developed to delay, conceal, or lessen your stuttering.

Making it a habit to refrain from avoiding, delaying, or substituting is crucial. Your avoidance habits may be to blame for a lot of your problems. Although they provide solace momentarily, such behaviors ultimately feed your concerns and make things worse. For instance, if the phone rings and you ignore it out of worry that you won't be able to speak clearly, ignoring the circumstance will simply serve to increase your fear of answering the phone.

You should try your best to avoid avoiding speaking opportunities, dodging social circumstances, giving up speech attempts or leaving the scene of approaching problems, substituting words, or using postponements to overcome fear. Don't steer clear of words you could stutter on.

Although many experts believe that non-avoidance will provide you with more relief than any other form of therapy, this can be a truly difficult task. Avoidances have been compared to a pump that draws fear from a reservoir. It would be beneficial if you could cultivate the mindset that you will actively seek out and get rid of avoidances. If you can develop the habit of facing your fears head-on without giving yourself any time to rationalize them away, you will eventually experience this feeling. Establishing avoidance-free speaking is very crucial for the stutterer.

6. Maintaining eye contact with the person you are conversing with.

You could be doing this already, but if not, begin by naturally staring your listener in the eye more or less consistently. You should pay extra attention to avoiding averting your gaze when you stutter or anticipate doing so.

Many people who stutter have a propensity to avoid looking at their listener when stuttering, perhaps because they are ashamed of their speech impediment. Continuously maintaining normal eye contact will help to lessen feelings of guilt and embarrassment. Focus on maintaining healthy, normal eye contact if you don't already.

7. Examine and pinpoint the incorrect motions your speaking muscles are making when you stutter.

Your ability to pinpoint precisely what your speech muscles are doing incorrectly when you stammer is a crucial and very significant component of this approach. Finding out what you are doing incorrectly or needlessly that needs to be changed or fixed is part of this. To reiterate, you must identify the erroneous things you are having your speech muscles perform to repair them. This is because when you stutter, you are using your muscles incorrectly.

Utilizing such an examination is an important aspect of therapy. We strongly advise that you observe the action of your speaking muscles and adhere to this rule. You can then repeat it to compare it to your natural speech when you speak without trouble.

There are several methods for self-observation. One option would be to either stammer slowly enough to give you time to feel what is occurring or to hang onto your stuttering blocks long enough to figure out what you are doing.

When making phone calls, you might also look in the mirror at yourself, play back a tape recording of your words, etc.

Or, if video equipment is accessible, it would be beneficial to have videotapes of your stuttering created. Being able to analyze what you are doing gives you a tremendous tool to focus on improving what you are doing incorrectly. It can be enlightening and inspiring to see and hear yourself stutter.

It will take guts to take these steps, but you need this knowledge to assist you address your issue so that you are fully aware of what has to be changed or fixed. The ability to feel, see, and hear your stuttering should be possible. You will be able to respond to the following three queries using this knowledge:

•What am I doing?

•Why am I acting this way?

•What else can I do?

8) Use block correction techniques to change or get rid of your aberrant speech muscle stuttering behavior.

Making significant progress may depend on your ability to effectively operate these processes. These practical techniques include

☐ A post-block correction that outlines what to do in response to a stuttering block once it has happened.

☐ An in-block corrective that outlines what to do in response to a block as it develops.

☐ a pre-block correction, for which you must make plans and get ready so that it won't happen.

They use the understanding they have received by researching your blocking issues, as stated in Rule 7, to assist you in gaining a sense of control. These should only be used after you have researched and determined what is abnormal about your speech mechanism when you stammer.

9. Always speak while moving forward.

Unless you deliberately repeat something to make a point. If you stutter, try to move forward as you stutter so that you don't hold or repeat any sounds. When trying to get through a word, some stutterers have a habit of repeating difficult sounds (g-g-g-girl, etc.)

There is no purpose in holding or repeating sounds or words once you have begun to express them. Any inclination to retain a block, extend, or repeat sounds or words on which difficulties are anticipated will be countered by keeping your speech flowing.

The goal is to continuously advance from one word or sound to the next with your voice. Plan to use a lengthy easy onset on the initial sound and the transition to the following sound when you expect problems with a word, but keep the voice moving ahead.

In other words, try to avoid repeating or going back and forth when speaking. You might be able to go past a block by going back to gain a running start, but you'll never get very far. So try your best never to hold or repeat sounds or words unless you are doing so on purpose to highlight a word or notion. Until you hear and see yourself on camera, you might not understand what you are doing.

10. Strive to speak with a firm voice, inflection, and melody without seeming forced or artificial.

Avoid speaking in a monotone and keep your volume and speaking rate varied. Speak melodiously while avoiding sounding forced. Talking will be more enjoyable and soothing if you use natural expressions and vary your tone and rate.

11. Pay close attention to your fluency

Don't limit your awareness to your stutter. When you speak fluently, listen to yourself. You must be aware of and recall your enjoyable and fruitful public speaking experiences. To increase your confidence, mentally practice effective speaking scenarios and experience your fluency.

Remind yourself that you are capable of speaking with ease. Spend some time talking or reading to yourself while you're alone and at ease to help yourself achieve that feeling. Work on some of this while gazing in the mirror. Keep in mind as you're doing it that you can speak normally and effortlessly without any effort on your part.

12. Make an effort to speak as much as possible

Talk as often as you can while working on this program since you will need every opportunity to practice the suggested procedures. This does not imply that you should be a nuisance, but rather that you should speak up more as you have probably been quiet for too long. When you want to, speak up. If there aren't any chances to talk, you should try to make some. Make your views known to others. If no one will listen, you can always call someone. Ask a question over the phone to a department shop.

These are the fundamental guidelines that should direct your speech and actions. They briefly describe the techniques that should help you control your problem. The later chapters will provide a more thorough explanation of how to adhere to these standards. Therefore, it is highly recommended that you read and learn each chapter associated with each rule.

5

Setting Goals

It can be difficult to work on reducing or changing your stutter since you will have to face challenges that you have previously avoided. Remember that you have the power to change your behavior and that stuttering is something you cause, not something that just happens to you. You'll notice that your emotional responses will alter as you alter your speaking style. When this occurs, it will be simpler to alter your speaking style.

Develop a Hierarchy

Let's address the issue. How do you plan to accomplish these objectives? Plan to go at it casually yet methodically and resolutely. You might want to start by methodically working through each rule one at a time. Consider starting with the easiest one and moving on to the next one. Create a hierarchy of circumstances and tasks. In other words, start in the simplest position and work your way up. By doing this, you increase your confidence as you go.

List five to ten speaking scenarios, ranking them from the simplest to the most challenging. In the following circumstances, adhere to Ground Rule 1, **speaking slowly and deliberately**:

1. conversing with a pet or by yourself (easiest to do)
2. conversing with a close friend
3. placing an order at a restaurant
4. speaking on the phone with a friend
5. speaking on the phone with a stranger
6. engaging in discussion at work
7. Participation at work meetings (hardest)

The points given here might not be appropriate for you, so you will need to create your hierarchy.

Set Up a Daily Quota

Set a goal for yourself each day. Before moving on to step three—placing an order in a restaurant, you might wish to repeat step two—discussing with a close friend while speaking slowly and thoughtfully (Rule 1) for a few days or even weeks.

Collect at least one instance of each day that you follow a rule, then two consecutive days, three consecutive days, and so on. Write down all of your accomplishments in your workbook, possibly towards the end of the day before you go to bed. The idea is to consistently do it more or less at the same time every day.

Maximum and Minimum Objective

Set a minimum objective that you are confident you can do and a maximum that could sap your motivation but can still be accomplished when outlining your goals. Create the following, for instance, if the rule requires you to talk slowly and deliberately. (minimum objective) I will read aloud to myself for five minutes speaking slowly and deliberately. (Maximum objective) I will use it on multiple phone calls whether or not I stutter.

Record your performance each day, make sure you follow all the regulations, and then progressively raise your quota for the following days.

A CHART

	Minimum Objectives	Maximum Objectives	Achieved Results
Sunday			
Monday			
Tuesday			
Wednesday			
Thursday			
Friday			
Saturday			

Rewards

Setting up a method to reward oneself will be beneficial. Find something you enjoy doing, such as watching TV for an hour, reading a magazine for an hour, or eating a snack, and only allow yourself to do it once you have achieved a certain objective. Alternatively, after completing so many assignments, you can allow yourself to purchase something you truly need or want.

You may find it challenging to follow some of these recommendations because you are altering lifelong behaviors. Do not give up if you occasionally try some of them and fail. Others have faced challenges and overcome them. Give it some time. You will have achieved your goal in great measure even if you can merely learn to stutter with ease and out loud to lessen the stress and severity of your struggle behavior.

Equipment

Certain things can help you change your stuttering tendencies. One is a moveable, fair-sized mirror that you may place where you can carefully watch yourself while speaking on the phone.

You must keep a notebook on hand so that you can document your daily efforts. Additionally, it will be beneficial if you can rent a little tape recorder that you can take with you and use to capture your stuttering. Small recorders that are hardly larger than your hand are widely available and can be acquired for a pretty inexpensive price. If you don't hear yourself on tape, you might not be aware of what you are doing when you stutter.

It would be even more advantageous for you to use a videotape recorder if you can afford the cost. You can use it to record your speech for videos. This makes it possible for you to see and hear yourself while speaking, exactly like if you were on television.

The topic of how to get recordings will arise if you do purchase a tape recorder. We're hoping you can make it work. Put the recorder close by while making phone calls if you have problems speaking on the phone. Some stutterers have tried recording their chats while they go into stores to talk about buying products they're interested in. A recording should last at least five or 10 minutes.

When you listen to these recordings, you can learn what you are doing poorly. All recordings should be helpful, and it's crucial that you consistently keep track of your daily progress in your notebook by making notes about it there. The majority of these basic rules will be covered in the chapters that follow, along with how they may affect your stuttering and how naturally you speak.

6

Mastering Slow and Deliberate Speech

RULE 1

Whether or not you stutter, the first rule requires you to develop the practice of speaking slowly and thoughtfully. It is advised to do this for a few different reasons. It first creates a style of speaking that is commonly regarded and admired, and it next produces a more diversified, laid-back style of speaking that is more receptive to therapy-controlled methods.

Accept your stuttering for the time being, commit to always speaking slowly and thoughtfully. If you tend to speak rather quickly, you won't find it simple to do this. When you speak, it could be difficult to speak slowly but you will adjust with time.

Spending at least five to ten minutes a day alone training will be beneficial. You may read aloud to yourself gradually and slowly, similar to how you would speak to someone else.

Then, perhaps, consider a topic that you are knowledgeable about, and speak slowly and purposefully to yourself.

Try your best to never feel rushed when you are around other people. You could occasionally experience a rush of hurry and haste that borders on panic right before you are due to speak. You feel as though you are speaking under "time pressure" with no time to spare, and you feel compelled to speak rapidly without giving your words a deliberate and comfortable expression. Try your best to ignore the feeling of urgency.

When they are ashamed, stutterers are also more likely to fear silence. As a result, it is advised that you try experimenting with pausing sometimes when speaking. Briefly pause between words and between phrases when uttering a sentence. There is no rush—you might not be spending as much time as you believe—so take your time. People will wait to hear what you have to say until there is a fire. Leave them alone and take your time when saying "hello" on the phone. Pause! Give it some time.

If you have a tape recorder handy, this would be a good moment to record your voice, especially if you have not yet begun speaking by the advice of this first guideline.

Making a recording of how you typically stutter will provide crucial data for this program. For instance, listening to such a recording should assist you in figuring out what, if anything, has to be done to make you eligible for slow, deliberate speech. The subject of how to get a recording of your stuttering raises itself. When you make multiple phone conversations, you might put a microphone nearby if you have problems speaking on the phone.

After that, spend some time listening to the recordings. Did you speak slowly and purposefully? These recordings will be used afterward to help you practice your speech. Of course, if it were possible, having videotapes of your speech would be even more helpful for reviewing it. You may now see and hear yourself at the same time.

7

Stuttering with Ease and Confidence

RULE 2

This second rule is essentially important, and it advises you to practice stuttering easily without effort. It doesn't need you to quit stuttering, just do it calmly, smoothly, and by easing your tongue, lips, and jaw into the sounds of your words. "Easy onset" or making light touches with your speech muscles is a term that has been used occasionally.

By attempting to force trouble-free communication, nothing is accomplished. Instead, strive to keep a calm, easy-going demeanor with minimal strain. Avoid stumbling when speaking. Keeping an eye on the amount of air pressure in your mouth is one technique to determine if you are having trouble. Avoid letting it accumulate behind your lips or tongue. Try stuttering while keeping your lips open and your tongue away from your palate and gums. Why create a barrier in your mouth that causes the air pressure to rise significantly.

To some extent, attempts to force trouble-free speech are to blame for the majority of stuttering. Unfortunately, the structure of speech is too intricate to work well under duress. Therefore, your intensity and frequency of stuttering will decrease if you can follow this rule and allow yourself to stutter freely.

We also advise you to practice relaxing your speech muscles while you are alone yourself, however, this may be challenging to do. This requires you to deliberately stiffen up, especially around your mouth. Afterward, let go of the tension or lower it so you can feel the difference.

If you deliberately make the transition from the first sound of any word you fear to the next sound or sounds of that same feared word longer, it will also make it easier for you to speak.

It iis recommended that you only prolong the first sound of dreaded words here before transitioning to the following sound or sounds of the same feared phrases. This could entail delaying the slow transition to the following sound by as much as a second or more.

Certain dreaded consonant sounds simply cannot be prolonged. These consonant sounds, which include those of 'k,' 't,' 'd,' 'b,' 'p,' and so on are known as plosives. However, you should ease into such sounds with light interactions by extending the words' subsequent tones. For instance, when speaking the word "cat," lightly touch the 'k' sound before slowly transitioning to the vowel sound of the "a."

Spend five to ten minutes a day reading aloud to yourself to practice speaking clearly and comfortably. While reading, use a forceful voice yet loose, casual speech. The goal is to become accustomed to controlling your speech muscles lightly and gently, whether or not you stutter.

Then, of course, it is advised that you practice prolonging the first sounds of your most dreaded words. You most likely don't worry about having trouble reading by yourself. Nevertheless, while you read, you can notice some words that make you stammer frequently. When you reach these words, try experimenting by gradually extending the beginning sound and making a point of doing the same with the transition to the next sound.

Adjustment to this informal way of speaking can be difficult. You should utilize reminders since you will occasionally forget. For instance, you could attach a rubber band to your wrist or hang a sign that says, "Remember to stutter easily today," so that you are constantly reminded to focus your efforts on speaking easily while extending certain sounds of your feared words. You can also make a list of the instances during the day when you remembered to talk or forgot to talk at night.

It is a good idea to keep track of your progress in your workbook as you use these rules. Initially aim for one successful performance, then two consecutive ones, three consecutive ones, etc., until you can gather five listeners in a row to whom you have spoken slowly and easily, whether or not you stutter.

We hope you'll be able to become used to conversing easily while pronouncing some initial sounds and transitions longer. While following this advice alone won't cure your stuttering, it will help you feel less anxious and stressed, which will improve the quality of your speech.

8

Embracing Stuttering as Part of Your Identity

RULE 3

The third therapy recommendation urges you to develop an attitude of openness about your stuttering and to stop trying to hide it. If you're attempting to avoid being one, you might wonder why you should do that.

It is advised that you first establish an attitude of being willing to speak freely about your problem with others to go forward. You will minimize your anxiety about speaking difficulties by doing this.

As was previously said, if you are like the majority of stutterers, you feel embarrassed by your stutter. As a result, you make an effort to hide the fact that you stammer from other people. A dread of trouble when called upon to speak at particular times and under particular circumstances tends to develop as a result of this feeling of humiliation.

This worry of difficulties typically causes tightness or tension in your speech organs, which makes your trouble worse. Unfortunately, the way that a person's speaking apparatus functions makes it extremely challenging for him to function under stress. As a result, the frequency and intensity of your difficulties are typically proportional to your level of anxiety.

It is vital to torpedo a lot of your guilt and sensitivity to confront anxiety and stress, which are your deadliest adversaries. A stutterer may expend a lot of energy trying to conceal their issue. Some people create complex avoidance and disguise methods or even adopt a masquerade in the hopeless hope that the listener won't detect their stuttering. Simply said, this weight makes communication more challenging.

What does all that stress and worry accomplish for you? Nothing. Since it simply intensifies anxiety and worry, it only makes the situation worse. What can or ought to be done as a result? Even if you are not preoccupied with keeping your stutter a secret, it will be beneficial to let go of any worries you may have in this regard.

Although the solution is simple and straightforward, it's not easy. By being honest with people about your stuttering and giving up pretending to be a normal speaker, you can alleviate a lot of their worries and concerns. You shouldn't avoid completing this task. Create opportunities to freely disclose that you stutter to the people you hang out with and with whom you typically speak, and be prepared to discuss it with anyone.

You'll need to have the guts to do this, but it's necessary to lessen your sensitivity. It takes time and effort to alter your mental perspective on a situation, but the more effort you put into it, the more progress you'll make. In any case, stuttering is not a shame. You may believe that, but if you do, you are mistaken. Please resist letting your emotions undermine your efforts.

Start this task by speaking with close friends and family members before moving on to converse with random strangers.

Someone once said, *"It took me seventeen years before I would confess that I stuttered, either to myself or to anyone. I didn't want to admit that I was unique. But to take the first step toward creating a new and more rewarding identity is exactly what I had to do."*

For instance, you might confess to a friend that you stutter and that, to be honest, you've been ashamed of talking about it. And you need to be more open about your issue as you require their assistance. Any genuine buddy will value your candor and become more attached to you as a result. Additionally, you'll discover that stuttering is a topic of fascination. Inform them of it.

By doing this task, you'll release tension and learn to accept your stuttering as a condition you can manage with less guilt and embarrassment. This can significantly improve your situation and provide you the ability to approach your problem with a more balanced, wholesome, and objective mindset—something that all stutterers need.

Although you may fear that being open about your stutter may hurt your pride, it's more likely that you will feel proud of yourself for doing so. Furthermore, pretending all your life is useless.

Obviously, you won't be able to do this task in a couple of days. Making touch with people you know and implementing this advice will take some time. No matter how long it takes, developing a willingness to talk about your stuttering will help ease your tension and worry. It's not easy but taking this step will help you get rid of a lot of your anxiety and dread.

Stuttering Voluntarily

It is advised that you be open to intentionally experimenting with stuttering while working on the third rule. This typically helps stutterers feel less anxious and fearful. When you purposefully stutter, you are actively combating the stress that is exacerbating your issue by choosing to do what you fear.

The first sound or syllable of a phrase, or the word itself, should be repeated or briefly prolonged in cases of voluntary stuttering, also known as fake or faux stuttering. Only non-fearful words should be used, and it should be done in a relaxed, peaceful manner.

Instead of mimicking your stuttering pattern, try stuttering naturally and smoothly in a different way. It is preferable to stammer easily and calmly when doing so on purpose because you will be expected to analyze and learn about your own pattern afterward.

You must be sure to maintain your stuttering is completely voluntary, regardless of the style you choose. It is not advised to allow it to spiral out of control and become compulsive. Try speaking deliberately and slowly with short repetitions or prolongations that break up your regular pattern. Controlling the uncontrollable will make you feel more in control of yourself.

When you're alone by yourself, start by reading carefully out loud while adding simple repetitions or extensions. Later, incorporate it into discussions with other people. Create assignments for yourself where you must voluntarily stutter. For instance, enter a store and pose as a customer while asking the salesperson how much various things will cost. Make the blocks simple but clear. Stuttering while maintaining eye contact is important. You should also make sure to only stutter on words you are not afraid of.

Your embarrassment may lessen if you stutter voluntarily. It will get simpler the more you can commit to doing it and experience doing it. Strive to avoid getting emotionally invested and be willing to stutter.

Do your best for several reasons. It is one method to acknowledge that you stutter. Additionally, you can observe how others respond to stuttering and learn that most people are kind and tolerant of others. Additionally, it will make you feel good about yourself for having the confidence to approach your issue head-on.

It also helps if you add some humor or are willing to make light of your stammer. Additionally, doing this lessens sensitivity. You might, for instance, occasionally mention that you stammer or make a lighthearted comment about it, such as saying that if you didn't talk, you wouldn't stutter, or say something like. *"We are experiencing technical difficulties and there might be a brief intermission."* These comments don't seem to be very funny, do they? They probably aren't, but to someone who does not stutter, they might be.

Developing a sense of humor about your struggle is beneficial. At the same time, avoid going too far and falsely portraying your stuttering as hilarious while secretly feeling awful about it, as some stutterers have done.

9

Eradicating Secondary Symptoms

RULE 4

This fourth tip advises you to get rid of—that is, quit doing—any extraneous actions or mannerisms that you might use to stutter or avoid difficulties. Even though most stutterers exhibit these strange tendencies, it's possible that you don't.

The abnormal use of your speaking muscles or mechanism, which is dealt with in rule 7, is not covered by this rule. It alludes to additional obvious, pointless, or auxiliary body movements that may define the specific pattern of your stuttering.

They are what speech therapists refer to as secondary symptoms, and they include physical mannerisms like eye blinking, fixations, grimaces, protrusions or postures of the mouth, covering your mouth with your hand, head movements or scratching, jaw jerks, ear pulling, finger-snapping or tapping, coin jingling, knee-slapping, foot tapping or shuffling, hand movements, or other actions that are not necessary for the production of speech.

These erratic behaviors may have started because you once thought they would help you get beyond a barrier or keep you out of trouble. However, they might now have merged with the stuttering itself. Eliminating any such unneeded and undesirable acts can make you happier.

You may not be responsible for doing such things, but you still need to break whatever bad habits you may have. It is crucial to learn how to control and adjust them. However, you obviously need to figure out what you do before you can attack them. This entails paying attention to how you stutter or attempt not to stutter. Since these routines are typically automatic and unconscious, you might not even be aware of the symptoms as they develop.

Examining oneself and becoming completely aware of the patterns that one has developed over time to get through challenging situations is difficult. Even though you cannot see yourself stutter, you should be able to feel it. You can also ask a close friend or family member to keep an eye out for your stuttering and take notes once you've described what to look for.

You could start by selecting a few specific speaking scenarios that will happen today or tomorrow in advance. Commit to paying close attention to yourself during these times. Be mindful of any motions you make when stuttering or anticipating doing so. Disregard whatever movements you might normally make, but make sure they are genuine and not intended to speed up your speaking or break a stutter.

Here's where a mirror, especially a full-length mirror, will help you see yourself more clearly. Make some phone calls while looking in the mirror if you have trouble speaking on the phone. Take note of any unusual postures or motions that go along with your stuttering. None of these should be skipped. Make some very uncomfortable and stressful phone calls to double-check, which will put pressure on you. Make a list of the symptoms in your workbook after each situation.

A prominent secondary symptom should be easy to recognize and list, but others might be a little harder to pick out. Stutterers can fail to notice behaviors that are clear to others. If you don't stammer or don't anticipate it, you might be startled to discover yourself doing something you wouldn't normally do. Make it a point to observe yourself as closely as you can when applying this guideline. Of course, recording your speech on video would be even more helpful in understanding your secondary symptoms.

This recommendation does not imply that a stutterer should cease utilizing any common gestures he may have developed a habit of using to emphasize or add expression to his speech. As long as it is not timed to a rhythm or the pace of one's speech, typical gesturing is welcomed.

Any subsequent symptoms you may experience should be completely eliminated. By doing this, you will be removing crutches that may have initially assisted you in spreading the word but cannot provide long-term relief.

Working on Secondary Symptoms

How do you stop this kind of behavior? It might not be simple. Such behavior can occasionally become so compulsive that quitting becomes nearly impossible. But if you set your mind to it, you can stop it. Willpower alone won't help you quit stuttering, but if you're persistent, you can discipline yourself to stop the secondary symptoms. But one needs to approach it methodically.

Unfortunately, no stutterer experiences the same secondary symptoms consistently. You might make a timing movement, blow your nose, swing your arms, stick out your lips, jingle your coins, or blink your eyes. Anything might happen. Additionally, other people's issues might not be the same as yours; nevertheless, as they will just be used as examples and the concepts of correction stated here should apply to all such stuttering habits or tactics, they don't need to differ from yours.

So let's begin by choosing a movement that you make that you would like to modify. It is best to focus on only one at a time, even if there are several. Making such movements intentionally while remaining silent is one approach to begin controlling it. For instance, it is advised to practice swinging your arm purposefully when by yourself and not speaking if you have a propensity of doing so when trying to chat. After that, start talking to yourself and swinging your arm in different directions so you can feel yourself changing what you're doing deliberately.

Or, for example, if you naturally blink your eyes, do it on purpose while you're by yourself and not talking. Then, when speaking to oneself, consciously and purposefully alter the blink's timing or pace. This method of solving such issues requires that you carry out these actions with intention and focus. Such a habit will be simpler to control or manage if it is brought under conscious control.

Until you are confident that you are the master and can skip it entirely, practice putting these behaviors under control in situations that cause worry. The fundamental concept is to make the behavior voluntary while it is happening, to vary it deliberately, to shorten its time, and then to stutter on the word when it isn't happening. If you're committed to changing, you can get rid of these habits.

You might be interested in learning how one stutterer got rid of the somewhat unsightly secondary symptom of tapping his foot. This stutterer had a habit of tapping his foot in time with the word or syllable when he stumbled. He chose certain speaking scenarios and counted how many times he tapped his foot when stuttering to determine how bad it was and exactly what he was doing. He found that when he was under stress, they typically appeared in particular words or noises, which was extremely tough for him to achieve. Eventually, he was able to count them.

Then, he experimented more with over-tapping than usual. When he did not stutter, he also deliberately practiced tapping, albeit he had to be especially cautious to ensure that it was done voluntarily. Of course, the goal was to give him conscious control over his compulsive tapping.

Then, by tapping in a different manner than usual when he was stuttering, he practiced changing his tapping technique. To give himself the impression that he had control over things, he would prepare his variations in advance. Do you get it now? It's crucial to look into every last detail of a secondary symptom in order to try and eliminate it. Before you can hope to triumph over any such habit, you must be aware of what you are doing. As you become more aware of this, you should start to behave differently. When you are not stuttering, it is always beneficial to deliberately act out your symptoms (whatever it may be).

Bringing it under conscious control and converting it from an unintentional movement to an intentional movement is the key to getting rid of it. Restart if you forget and discover that you are losing control. Change up your delivery on purpose as you speak. Practice taking charge in anxiety-provoking circumstances until you feel confident that you are the master and can forego it entirely.

The fundamental concept is to make the behavior voluntary while it is happening, to vary it deliberately, to lessen its time, and then to stutter on the word when it isn't happening. If you're committed to changing, you can get rid of these habits.

10

Tackling Avoidances, Delays, and Substitutes

RULE 5

This very crucial rule requires you to make a genuine attempt to quit any avoidance, substitute, or postponement habits you may have developed to delay, conceal, or lessen your stuttering. You must cultivate avoidance-free speaking because it is crucial.

This might be a bigger issue than you believe because a stutterer often exhibits odd behavior to delay or avoid what he perceives as dangerous situations. Many stutterers believe that to reduce the risk of becoming stuck, they must always be prepared for everything.

Avoidances may provide solace momentarily, but they will ultimately make your anxieties worse and put you in more difficulties. Until time runs out or their effectiveness wanes, they keep it stimulated. Successful avoidances will keep stuttering alive.

Why not avoid speaking your name or picking up the phone if you think you might stutter while doing so? Or then, why isn't it okay to, at the very least, put off doing something? Or why not use a word that is easier to pronounce instead of one on which you could stumble? Why not?

There is one compelling reason not to carry out these actions, and it is a good one. The more you practice avoiding, delaying, or replacing, the more you'll continue to use these crutches to get out of difficulties, which will just feed your stuttering dread. Why do we let dread grow? The stutterer wants his concerns to be lessened, not strengthened, if there is one thing more than anything else. Avoidance simply serves to increase stuttering anxiety.

Stutterers sometimes use a variety of avoidance techniques to lessen or avoid problems, including avoiding speaking situations, avoiding social interactions or phone calls, using secondary symptoms or exaggerated gestures, speaking more quickly, repeating words or going back to get a head start, speaking in a monotone or sing-song voice, varying the pitch or intensity of the voice, acting in an unnaturally aggressive manner, and more.

Postponements include a variety of stalling techniques like clearing the throat, swallowing, coughing, blowing the nose, inserting extra words like "you know" "I mean" or "that is," or overusing interjections like "uh," "er," "well," etc. Use synonyms, simple words, or other phrases in place of those you believe you could be blocked from using. Or you could use other techniques or approach a feared phrase from a different angle. Avoidance tactics include postponements and substitutions.

As has been stated, the stutterer stutters when they are attempting not to stutter. The number of problems you experience would much decrease if you could voluntarily adopt an attitude of not seeking to hide or avoid. This phase might not be simple and will demand focused effort. You should read, research, and complete assignments like those outlined in the next part.

Working on Avoidances

Although following this guideline and giving up all avoidance behaviors may be difficult, many experts believe that this approach will be more effective for you than any other method of therapy. So let's make a concerted effort to cease any avoidance behaviors or techniques you may have picked up to delay, conceal, or lessen your stuttering.

To determine what has to be addressed, you should start by determining how frequently, when, and to what extent you might use avoidances. Plan to start your day by closely observing yourself throughout the day to learn and recognize any avoidance techniques you may be doing.

Examine your day's thoughts and actions, and record both what you did and why in your workbook. Keep track of the activities you took or didn't take that were affected by your desire to stay out of trouble. Keep track of this data for several days. You'll be shocked by how often you put off, cancel, or substitute.

After gathering this data, you should get to work attempting to stop all such behaviors. A progressive approach could be preferable because it might be too challenging to try to work on them all at once, however, that is a matter of your judgment. Anyway, choose one avoidance behavior that you know is bad and resolve to improve on it. Make a concerted attempt to break only that one particular habit. Approach things as methodically as you can. To ensure that it receives enough attention so that you won't use it any longer, you'll need to keep an eye on yourself for a while. Keep a record of both your successes and mistakes. Don't allow the challenges you face to demotivate you since these changes don't just happen. Keep working on the task.

Decide, for example, not to use word substitutions. You'll need to keep a close eye on yourself because you might be doing this regularly. One method for solving a replacement problem is to purposefully employ words that you know would make you stutter. Say what needs to be said, and if you stammer, keep going. The exact words you're about to speak should be written out. And repeat them without modification or substitution.

Similarly, you should not remain silent while claiming to think of an answer, pretend to not hear when someone talks to you, or claim to not know when you are aware of something. You shouldn't shun speaking opportunities, shirk social obligations, give up on speech attempts, or flee the scene of potential trouble either.

You could try chatting more often in threatening circumstances as a challenge. Maybe every day, look for one frightening circumstance to face head-on. Just be careful not to back down and avoid it after you have made up your mind to do so. After that, describe the encounter in writing.

You don't have to volunteer to give talks in front of people, but you will feel better about yourself if you purposefully participate in more speaking opportunities. For instance, even if you are aware of the fare, ask the bus driver. Or say "good morning" when you previously kept quiet to a store clerk.

You will be encouraged to take part in activities that present a challenge as you advance. You must speak as much as you can. You'll have to quit escaping at some point. The time to stand and fight is right now. Actually, by actively seeking out feared phrases and putting yourself in challenging situations, you will experience a sense of accomplishment. The less you avoid, the more self-assurance you'll have in your ability to be a decent and deserving individual. In the routine exchanges of life, you should speak up rather than back down.

Using a Telephone

Has the phone recently rung? While you shouldn't eject others to take the call, if you would naturally be the one to do so, do so. This could help you face your worst fear. You may tell yourself it's too much and you just can't handle it. You cannot expect to spend your entire life avoiding the phone, even if you are not attempting to conquer your stutter. You'll need to pick up the phone and speak at some point. The harder it will be the longer you put it off.

On the other hand, it's possible that you don't mind talking on the phone as long as you have other issues. Let's assume that you did answer the call you received earlier and spoke with the caller. When you encountered a term in the conversation that you anticipated stuttering on, did you immediately consider a different way to express it? Maybe you did. If that's the case, you've built another stone on your fear's wall.

What did you do, incidentally, when you ran into so-and-so the other day and were worried you would stammer when you spoke to him? How did you manage to speak with him? Did you move to the other side of the room, run away from him, or just remain silent? Unfortunately, we are unaware of the kinds of interactions or gatherings you avoid.

As we previously stated, make a habit of speaking up whenever you come across typical circumstances when you would like to. It's important to consider both your viewpoint and the next person's. Use any words that come to mind. To prevent stuttering, prepare to speak your thoughts aloud without alterations or substitutes. You will develop self-confidence if you are determined to approach your issues in this manner.

Spend time planning how not to avoid problems now that you have the habit of planning how to avoid trouble. Sometimes you might not follow through, but if that happens, you should make up for it by putting yourself in additional or similar situations where you're worried you might stumble. Everyone loses sometimes, but they can always recover. In any case, when it comes to any such assignments, be honest with yourself. You are only deceiving yourself if you give an alibi.

Here's how one stutterer describes what he did to try and lessen the avoidances that were continually feeding his concerns.

"I've been using every trick in the book for years to prevent stuttering or cover it up when it does occur. Even though I typically get away with it, I still live in constant anxiety that eventually my identity would be revealed, which is usually the case. The toughest part of it, however, is that I have to maintain continual watch, constantly evaluating circumstances and words for telltale indicators of impending danger. I am so weary of constantly having to prepare to avoid, duck, and cover up my dread.

"Anyway, I decided to confront the matter head-on today since I was so utterly fed up. I started by avoiding conversation by having breakfast in a cafe instead of the usual cafeteria. Three times I circled the cafe before summoning the confidence to enter, but I did so at last.

I tried practicing my order and adjusting my choices to avoid stuttering, but I was so ashamed of my frailty that when the waitress arrived, I just blurted out "c-c-c-cheese tacos and eggs!" and purposefully stumbled on the cheese. She didn't flinch when I stared at her. I was merely asked whether I wanted coffee, to which I replied, "c-c-c-cheese tacos, eggs and coffee." You have no idea how amazing I felt. I had, for once, not been a coward. They can ignore it if they don't like it! I felt strong, not weak, and the cheese tacos and eggs were delicious.

"After breakfast, I had such positive self-esteem that I decided to answer the phone, which has always been my worst worry. In the normal course of things, I might have gone to the bus terminal rather than called to ask when the buses to Trenton were scheduled to depart. I was so terrified of the phone that I hung up twice when they answered the call without saying anything. I was in such a panic that I hardly knew where to begin even if I could have.

"Consequently, I sat down and wrote, "When do the buses depart for Trenton this afternoon?" I placed the mirror next to the phone so I could see myself while dialing, uttered the number aloud, and then hung up. Even though I didn't stutter as much as I had anticipated, I had to repeat myself since the clerk didn't understand the first time, but I still managed to get the information I required. Afterward, I felt completely spent yet victorious."

11

Maintaining Eye Contact During Communication

RULE 6

Like many stutterers do , you probably avoid looking people in the eyes when you speak to them. Most likely, if you pay close attention to yourself, you will notice that you typically avert your eyes, especially when you are stuttering or anticipating a block. Additionally, doing this tends to make you feel more ashamed or embarrassed about your situation.

While maintaining eye contact won't stop your stuttering by itself, it will assist lessen feelings of shyness and generally boost your confidence. This sensitivity is a major contributor to the tension that either starts or intensifies your problem. This recommendation, therefore, urges you to develop the practice of making eye contact with your audience.

This doesn't imply that you must fix your gaze on the person you are speaking to, but you should nonetheless maintain constant eye contact with the other person. Before you start speaking, make eye contact and maintain it naturally. Try your hardest to maintain eye contact, especially if you stutter or anticipate doing so.

You may already make eye contact, but it's more likely that you avoid it out of embarrassment. Do your best, to be honest with yourself, but keep in mind that it can be challenging to monitor yourself. You could ask a close friend or family member to listen while you talk to see if they notice whether you avert your gaze before or after stuttering.

You may be averting your gaze out of concern for your listener's sympathy, rejection, or impatience. This is unlikely to be accurate. Making eye contact with your listener will help you determine whether your anxieties are justified and should also reassure them. Additionally, by maintaining eye contact, you might show that you embrace rather than dismiss your stuttering as an issue that needs to be fixed. By turning your head aside, you are rejecting the issue.

Anyhow, make it a practice to keep up good eye contact. It will help you fight emotions of inferiority and self-consciousness, so you'll feel better for doing it. Its use is advised by therapists while attempting to assist bashful individuals. Eye contact is always helpful in interpersonal communication, even if you don't stutter. Effective speakers employ it naturally.

You don't need to squint or hang your head in shame, which is perhaps what you are doing when you do. We hope that you can come to believe that you are just as capable as the next individual. Try your best to maintain a straight face before the world.

How to Maintain Eye Contact

You might have more trouble than you think carrying out this guideline. Many stutterers have developed such extreme shyness that it is challenging for them to look someone in the eye directly when they are stuttering. As you try the ensuing steps, it is advised that you carefully double-check your actions.

Start by feigning an easy block when alone and glancing in the mirror. Do you look away from yourself or do you maintain eye contact? Try it several times while maintaining eye contact. Do it after making a strong block. If you discover that you cannot maintain eye contact before and during the block, practice until you can, then carry on.

Then, while experiencing genuine blocks, make some phone calls while gazing in the mirror. Keep an eye on yourself until you can speak without looking away for five or more genuine stutters. This is a crucial step to properly complete this program.

It will be simpler for you to keep eye contact while speaking in casual conversation as you gain confidence. This does not imply that you must scowl or concentrate your gaze on your audience; rather, you should maintain eye contact with them while they are turning away from you. Compile one, two, and then three instances where you make eye contact while stuttering when speaking to others. Then add ten more times.

It is advised that you either write down the names and eye colors of 10 persons with whom you have stuttered or write down ten or more words on which you have stuttered without breaking normal, natural eye contact, to demonstrate that you have followed through.

Use your creativity to come up with other pertinent assignments. You'll feel better if you practice making nice, natural eye contact while speaking on all occasions going forward. Knowing that you can follow this rule will make you feel good and improve your conversational skills.

12

Uncovering Your Speech Habits and Behaviors

RULE 7

Discovering precisely what you are doing with your speech mechanism when you are experiencing difficulty is a crucial component of this therapeutic approach. As a result, you are urged to recognize and experience the improper articulatory movements and contacts that you make when you stutter.

The more you observe how you become blocked on particular sounds or words, the more you'll come to understand that there are ways to get through them effortlessly. To put it another way, the more closely you examine your poor speaking habits, the more likely you are to benefit from controls that will change or stop your unnatural or unneeded activities.

You may detest even the thought of analyzing your stutter, yet it's crucial to know this information. Most likely, you are just vaguely aware of how you stutter and are unable to reproduce your anomalies. You may only be aware of the fact that you occasionally speak freely and occasionally find yourself hopelessly stumped.

In any event, we want you to have a sense of how the muscles that govern your breath, mouth, lips, and tongue behave so that you can learn how to mimic your stuttering and compare their behavior to that of when you speak normally. As part of your assignments, you'll research how your speech muscles assemble speech sounds and words when you stutter vs how they behave normally when you talk naturally.

You will be asked to deliberately stutter while copying your typical pattern and watching yourself in the mirror to determine this. Furthermore, if you have ever been able to have recordings or videos of your stuttering made, these will be a huge help. It will be simpler for you to learn how to alter or rectify what you have been doing if you can both hear and see yourself stutter.

Even though these assignments may appear unusual and uncomfortable, if you face your problem head-on and attempt to solve it, improvement is still achievable. Others can tolerate your stutter if they can see and hear it. It's not quite as horrible as you think.

Analyzing Your Blocks' Pattern

To acquire a sensation or sense of awareness of the movement and locations of your speech mechanism when you stutter, you are recommended to conduct a self-examination and explore your obstructions. This is especially true of the activities you do that are unneeded and out of the ordinary.

How do you go about doing this self-analysis? To gain a sense of what's going on, stutter incredibly slowly as you block. This refers to stuttering slowly rather than speaking slowly. Stuttering is a good strategy to use when you sense problems coming, but make sure you do it slowly so you can feel exactly what is wrong with your speech muscles.

To become aware of what is happening in those sounds that are problematic for you, keep doing this and trying to sense what happens when you block and when switching to the next sound. Note and document everything that stands out as different or superfluous.

When you run into problems, repeating your blocks is another technique to obtain this knowledge. Be brave and stammer on them once more. However, the second time, move through the block so slowly that you can feel your speaking muscles tensing up.

Using Mirror to Check Your Stutter

If you have problems speaking on the phone, using a mirror gives you a great chance to see what you are doing incorrectly when you stammer. Place the mirror adjacent to the phone, where you can carefully monitor your face.

Naturally, make a few phone calls after that. If no one is available, you can always call businesses for information while keeping an eye on your stuttering. Then, as you speak, pay close attention to the motions of your mouth, body, etc., and point out any unusual or unnatural movements of your speech muscles.

Again, if you can deliberately stutter slowly, you will have a better opportunity of observing what is happening.

Additionally, if you can, freeze your movement as you block to make any out-of-place positions more evident. You require this knowledge in order to mimic any peculiar moves.

Pick a term that bothers you when you are finished talking on the phone. It may be, for instance, your name. Anyhow, a word like that will contain a sound that you usually block.

Stutter on the word purposefully while you look at yourself in the mirror, mimicking the way you get stuck, and try to make the block as natural-looking as you can. Repeat the block a second time, this time stuttering only on the sound or syllable, and do so in a very slow motion. It could be challenging to reduce the stuttering but keep trying until you can do it gently.

Now, to compare the two, speak the same sound correctly this time, trying to feel what happens when you do so while not stuttering while gazing in the mirror. Repeat saying the syllable slowly enough times that you start to notice how different it feels when you block on it versus when you speak it effortlessly. Make a list of the actions you take that are unusual, unneeded, or odd when you stammer.

Although it could seem complicated, it shouldn't be that challenging because you'll probably discover that your stuttering style doesn't vary all that much. Given that most stutterers tend to repeat the same abnormal postures or speech muscle movements each time they stutter, you may discover that your pattern of stuttering is more or less uniform and consistent.

Using Tape Recorder

To learn how you stutter so that you can mimic it, a tape recorder can be useful. Even if its application is obvious, people are usually curious to see how it works. The recorder can be discreet, compact, and not draw attention to itself.

You may have already recorded discussions with friends and relatives. You should also take the recorder outside and use it to make additional recordings while you are moving about. Make an effort to strike up conversations with strangers if you don't want to chat with individuals you know, even if it's just to get directions or the time of day while you're filming.

Making recordings of phone calls in front of a mirror while occasionally freezing your articulations or continuing your repeats, etc., is advised if you have problems speaking on the phone. Of course, once you've taped talks, you should play them again and listen to what was said. To better comprehend what happened, play the tapes slowly in the areas where you had problems.

Repeat this several times, pantomiming or mimicking your speech patterns as you listen to the audio. When you stammer, you need to be able to see, hear, and reproduce what you are doing. Even if you don't have a recorder, try your hardest to get this right so you can grasp the scenario much better.

Of course, it is even more helpful if you can arrange to have video recordings of your stuttering activities recorded. You can see and hear what you are doing incorrectly and what has to be changed by watching such films. It gives you the best opportunity to research your challenge. Getting such a recording is advised.

You can compare the activity of your speech muscles with what they do when you talk fluently once you have identified what you are letting them do abnormally when you stammer. This phase could take some time to complete, but keep going until you feel like you understand what your stutterers do wrong.

It requires rigorous study to work toward obtaining the information required for this phase, but the more awareness you have of your challenge, the simpler it will be to overcome. Read the next section outlining how to evaluate in depth what a stutterer does with his speech mechanism when he has trouble for more detailed examples of how you can monitor your speech muscle actions.

This section provides detailed instructions on how to analyze your mistakes. You can use this knowledge to create the block corrections that are discussed in the next chapters.

13

Techniques for Analyzing Your Speech Mechanism During Difficulties

This chapter goes into great detail on how to sense your blocks and understand them so you can fix your mistakes. Unfortunately, we are unable to obtain specific information on what transpires in your case. However, we'll outline a few different types of stuttering behavior that might occur when particular consonant sounds are made. You'll have a better notion of how to approach your difficulties after reading this.

It should be remembered that every vocal utterance, whether it be singing or speaking, consists of a variety of distinct sounds that are then joined to form words. To put it another way, when you speak, you make the sounds that make up words. For the sake of simplicity, these sounds will be referred to as vowel and consonant sounds, with vowel sounds denoting 'a,' 'e,' 'i,' 'o,' 'u,' etc., and consonant sounds denoting 'b,' 'c,' 'd,' 'f' etc.

You might believe that you are blocking a word when you stutter. That is accurate, however, you are blocking more particularly on a sound in that word or when switching from one sound to the next in that word. Using a straightforward example, if you stutter saying "d-d-d-doll," you aren't simply blocking the "d" sound because you've already made it, but you are also having problems moving from the "d" sound to the rest of the word.

The transition from one sound to the next is a challenge for many stutterers. You might discover, among other things, that your airflow is irregular or jerky, that you exhale all of your air first before trying to speak, that you use interjections or starter noises, that your lips are stuck together and you are unable to open them, that your tongue is stuck to the roof of your mouth, that you use rapid-fire repetitions or just repeat sounds, that your jaw trembles, that you prolong certain sounds, etc.

Trying to Say a Name

Let's test your ability to make a sample consonant sound using your speech muscles. Assume that your name is Paul and that you struggle particularly with the 'p' sound and the change from one sound to the next.

(Almost every stutterer has difficulty pronouncing his own name, especially when asked to do so in front of a higher-up.)

Just so you know, the "p" sound is referred to as a "labial plosive." Correctly creating this type of sound requires swiftly parting your lips after shutting them and building up a small amount of air pressure. Try producing the sound on your own.

Anyway, as you say your name with a lot of strain in front of the mirror, stammer horribly on the 'p' sound. Repeat the process of stuttering on it, but this time do it in incredibly slow motion so you can feel what your speech muscles are doing when you block. Repeat several times.

What transpired, and what did you learn? You undoubtedly have too much anxiety, but where was it mostly concentrated? It's possible that there wasn't any airflow since your thick lips blocked the airway.

You may have hummed and hawed instead of going straight for the 'p' sound, utilizing a variety of repetitious starting sounds like 'uh' or 'er' or 'well,' etc. Or perhaps you got stuck and had to start repeating a word. Your speaking muscles may have briefly frozen in a tight position as a result of the strain, preventing any sound.

Your lips or jaw may have vibrated somewhat, or the sound may have come out in a bounce pattern, repeating p-p-p-p, like a broken record. Alternatively, it's possible that your lips protruded or were compressed, causing a rapid tremor.

It's more likely that you are blocked by keeping your mouth closed. In other words, you made the sound of a 'p' with your lips so tightly closed that you were unable to open them and let the air out. You were making such firm, tight contact that you were unable to uncork your mouth. Are you familiar with these behaviors?

Of course, you aren't doing all of these things and encountering all of these issues, but you should note where and how you get stuck, using the letter "p" to remind yourself of what may be changed or removed.

To experience the difference between how you stutter on it and how you say it without stuttering, say your name several times in incredibly slow motion while standing stationary in front of your mirror. Feel the distinction.

Let's assume that the reason you had trouble with the 'p' sound was that you firmly or tightly compressed your lips together, blocking the sound. What can you do to break this habit, or what should you do?

To stop the pressure from building up, you can fix it by releasing or reducing the tension in your lips. Your lips should feel weak and floppy as you begin to enunciate your name. You should then actively control your movement such that your lips barely minimally touch as you pronounce the letter "p." An example of this is mild contact.

You need to manage the movement of your lip muscles so that they make light contact with no pressure at all. You can actively manage your lips' movement in this way to ensure that they only lightly contact while allowing air from your breath to pass between them. Make soft, loose contacts as often as possible to become used to controlling your lip movement during the 'p' sound.

To learn how to alter or control your speech muscle action, you must identify the specific articulative contacts or movements you produce when stuttering. To change any harmful habits you may have developed, you must do this. You'll discover that many of them are pretty simple to comprehend and may be changed or removed by using the remedial techniques discussed in the following chapters.

Others are more complicated, but if you carefully examine your poor speech patterns, you should be able to utilize controls to change or stop your unnatural or unneeded behaviors. You will become more aware that you should be able to go through a block without trouble the more you continue to observe how you stutter on the sounds and words with which you struggle and compare them with how you say them fluently.

The Outcome of Comparison

You'll see from this comparison that you must have been making extraneous speaking movements, which contribute to your difficulties. For the proper production of the sounds or words you are trying to utter, such movements would not be necessary. Therefore, now that you have studied and are aware of what these unnecessary or wasteful acts are, you may start working to stop them.

We wish we knew exactly what needs to be done in your situation, but we are unaware of the specific pattern of your stuttering. Unfortunately, the articulation of all sounds involves so many different detail variations that it would be difficult to list them all.

The following chapters will discuss how to use block corrections to change or rectify what is incorrect utilizing this knowledge. You will discover that you no longer need to stutter even though it is impossible to consciously manage all the speech motions required by applying these block repairs as instructed. We want to reiterate that stuttering is something you are doing and that you can alter or change it.

You can substitute a more appropriate response for your previous stuttering one. You don't have to struggle with barriers for the rest of your life and be miserable for yourself. Have confidence in your capacity to solve the issue.

14

Strategies for Correcting Blocks

RULE 8

As a result of your research in the previous chapter, it's likely that you now have a clearer understanding of exactly what your speech muscles have been doing abnormally when you stammer. The next logical step after learning this important information is to act to change or remedy what you have been doing unnecessarily or improperly.

It is advised that you practice block corrections. These three are intended to demonstrate to you how you can alter or alter what you are doing as you stammer. Additionally, they will help you manage the anxieties brought on by your fluency disturbances.

How to use these corrections is covered in the following three sections. The first one, "Post-Block Correction," goes into great depth about how to undo everything you have done improperly after experiencing a block. The best way to learn is to practice this first.

The "In-Block Correction" section that follows explains how to get out of a block that you might be in. The "Pre-Block Correction" section then describes how to get ready to proceed without incident through an anticipated block. That describes the last stage of this program and is the goal toward which your efforts have been aimed.

Post-Block Correction

Cancellation

One of the best methods you may utilize to learn how to stutter less badly is certainly this one. It is simple, yet it forces you to face and accept your stutter. When you get a block, use this post-block correction technique before moving on to your next sentence. It should be simpler to sense just what went wrong and how it needs to be changed at that point.

It is advised that you now put the outcomes of your research into how you stutter into action by honing these fixes, which are occasionally referred to as **cancellations.** Make every effort to carry out this. It gives you the chance to change your behavior right away to fix your mistakes.

The post-block adjustment functions, in brief, are as follows. You should pause momentarily after stuttering on a word to give yourself time to reflect, identify the trigger, and formulate a plan for fixing the problem. You are expected to overcorrect your uncoordinated speech muscle actions when making post-block repairs.

The course of events is described in the section that follows. Make sure you thoroughly comprehend the technique described in the explanation before putting it into practice when you stutter. The steps are shown by numbers in parentheses in order.

Action Sequence

The first thing you should do when you stammer on a word is

1. To finish saying the word that you blocked—that is, to say the word completely. Don't give up or try to avoid it by whatever means. Once the word has been spoken, you must then.

2. Possess the willpower to pause and come to a complete stop. The intermission is there to allow you time to consider your issue and pantomime a solution.

3. When you have finally stopped, Make an effort to loosen up your throat and other speech-related muscles. Feel your tongue drooping limply in the back of your mouth. Open your mouth slightly, as if you were about to drool, and let your lips hang slack. The trick is to notice how your breathing returns to normal as you start to feel the tension release.

4. Think back as you take a moment to unwind and then ask yourself what you did badly or abnormally that caused you to become fixated on that sound. You learned in the last chapter how to use your speech muscles to fix or repair faults you made while you blocked on various sounds.

5. Think about what went wrong when you stuttered using this information, and then consider what you can do to gradually correct or change the errors you made on this specific sound or word.

6. Then, to change your typical pattern of stuttering and go through the word, mentally practice or silently imitate how it would feel to have your mouth slowly make these repairs.

As you take time to consider your blocking issue and make plans for how to address it, it might seem to you that the person you are speaking to is losing interest in what you have to say. That is possible, but hold your ground and focus on working this post-block correction properly. Take your time as the pause needs to be long enough to achieve your goal of making your course of action.

7. Then and only then, repeat the word as you feel yourself making the repairs. After deciding what needs to be done to fix the mistakes you made, and after mentally rehearsing how it will feel to pronounce the word again while making these corrections.

8. But this time, smoothly and for a long time, pronounce the sound you blocked. You'll have more time to focus on feeling yourself repair or at least alter the speech muscle mistakes that caused you to stutter. And keep speaking smoothly so that you can gradually switch to the next sound.

Please remember to over-correct your incorrect speech muscle motion when speaking in this manner. Modify your typical blocking behavior when you hear a sound. If mild contact is required, for instance, press so softly that there is little to no contact. And pay more attention to the way the word feels when it is spoken rather than how it sounds.

Although it could seem like a long time, this post-block fix shouldn't take more than a few seconds. Less time will be needed the more you practice and improve at it. You will have plenty of opportunity to feel yourself making the necessary modifications if you move through the sound slowly and repeatedly while maintaining a flowing voice.

You don't have to feel bad about purposefully repeating your stuttering words. Others will be able to tell that you are determined to control your difficulties by the tiny delay and the cautious corrections. The majority of listeners are considerate by nature, and they will appreciate your efforts. You'll have plenty of chances to apply post-block corrections, so it could be helpful to practice them out loud when you're on your own.

Copying a stuttering block can be distressing. Your inclination could be to continue as is rather than modify the block, repeating the stammered word normally the second time. It should be noted, nevertheless, that if you do so, you will lose out on the significant advantage that comes with this process.

When you stutter, keep employing these corrections. You can improve your ability to move through a block by using them. They'll disrupt your stuttering pattern and give you more assurance in your capacity to control your speech.

As one person put it, *"It was pretty challenging to stutter and then wait to try again, but it's become better. Each time I did it, I gained more understanding of my stammer."*

In-Block Correction

Pull-Out

You learned how to stop stuttering after it started with the post-block repair. Now when you are in the middle of a block, it is suggested that you can utilize a somewhat similar technique to break out of it. This should be utilized when you need to ease out of a block that you are having trouble getting out of. What do you typically do if you find yourself suddenly feeling blocked?

You may have used some cunning strategy to get out of a situation like this, but it's more likely that you've simply been fumbling around, attempting to force your way out. It would be preferable to employ an organized technique termed an "in-block" correction, which is suitable for this therapeutic strategy.

So here is how it works. Avoid pausing or stopping to restart when you are in the middle of a block. The sound will be stabilized by slowing down a repetition, changing the repetition into a prolongation, smoothing out a tremor, or pulling out of a fixation as you ease out of the block. Instead, continue the stuttering, slowing it down and letting the block run its course.

By practicing this, you'll notice that altering the rate of your block while also learning to smooth out your stutter allows you to manage how long it lasts. Hold the stammering for as long as necessary to feel in control, identify your mistakes, and determine what needs to be changed to correct them. You should be aware of what you can do to correct your improper speech behavior based on your prior research.

Once you've realized this, stop prolonging or repeating your speech and, in slow motion, put into action the steps you determined would reverse or fix the improper speech muscle movement.

It would be preferable for you to perform a post-block correction to maintain the sensation that you are in control if for some reason you are unable to control your stutter and move out of the block as mentioned above. In any event, thanks to what you have discovered through your analysis and study of how you stammer, you should be able to remedy what you did incorrectly.

Pre-Block Correction

Formulaic Set

You must have diligently practiced and consistently used post-block and in-block adjustments when you stumbled by this point. You have fresh insight into how to react and how to proceed past a block in a planned way as a result of doing this. Now you should be able to stop stuttering immediately after it occurs.

However, because the procedure did not end the stuttering when it began, you might have thought that post-block repairs were equivalent to shutting the barn door after the animal was gone. Of course, you are correct, however since this training prepares you for the following action, you must receive it. You now need to understand how to prepare to stop your stuttering before it starts. 'Pre-block' rectification is the process of preventing blocks from happening.

Most of the time, you can predict potential problems before they arise. Stuttering is sometimes referred to as an "anticipatory struggle reaction" which essentially means that you anticipate difficulties and react by trying to escape them. Sometimes, there is no expectation and the blocks catch you off guard.

We suggest that you make use of the fact that you typically anticipate difficulties before it manifests. Doing so will offer you the chance to respond to the threat of trouble by anticipating it.

To overcome your stuttering in this stage, it is advised that you get out in front of a block and approach it in a novel and improved way by using a pre-block correction. Except for the fact that planning is done beforehand (pre) rather than after (post), this is comparable to the post-block adjustment.

When you anticipate stuttering on a word or sound, you should pause just before saying the word to plan how you will tackle it. This is known as the pre-block correction. And before you start speaking the word, you stop to consider how you typically stammer on the sound and determine what has to be changed to eliminate the mistakes you frequently make.

Although this procedure is identical to the post-block procedure, it is important that you carefully read the following instructions so you will understand exactly how it should be carried out. It is a crucial component of your therapy plan.

We describe in detail how these pre-block modifications should be applied to avoid any potential misunderstandings. You'll need to focus your attention on it. The steps in the technique are identified below

Action Sequence

When approaching a sound or word that you are afraid of, you should use a pre-block correction just as described above.

1. Pause; completely stop speaking as you approach the word and just before you begin to say it. This pause before saying the word provides you time to gather your thoughts, plan, and practice how you will respond to it.

The pause won't last long, and being willing to stop will show your listener and yourself that you are committed to taking charge of the situation. Even though it takes longer, if you stumble into the pause blindly, it might be less awkward than your stuttering.

2. When you have finished speaking, make an effort to relax your throat and the rest of the stiff voice mechanism. Try to imagine your tongue laying limp in the back of your mouth, your jaw slightly open, and your lips hanging loosely as if you were about to drool. Check to see if you can feel some looseness there.

3. Consider the past while you unwind and think about the weird things you often do when you hear that sound. What mistakes do you frequently make when stuttering on it?

Your research and study of your speech muscle action as well as your previous experience with post-block corrections should help you recall these mistakes.

4. To help you remove or alter the abnormalities you make when you block on it, use this review of the mistakes you typically do to determine what corrections you learned to put into practice to replace what you typically performed incorrectly when you stuttered on that sound.

5. Next course of action is to speak the entire word slowly and deliberately over a longer period of time, changing gently from one sound to the next, to simulate how it would feel in your mouth to apply these modifications. To avoid the mistakes you frequently make on that sound, you must mentally practice or pantomime how you will implement these alterations.

6. Say the word, making the necessary corrections as you practiced them, as soon as your breathing returns to normal—and not before.

7. But exaggerate the adjustments and articulate the sound and word in a sliding resonant extended manner, focusing more on how the word feels than how it sounds. You

shouldn't speak slowly in any other situations, even though the next few words might be affected.

Making the transition from the consonant sound to the vowel sound that follows is frequently problematic. The smooth transition is achieved by speaking the feared word in a leisurely, protracted manner while maintaining sound flow. Additionally, it gives you enough opportunity to practice correcting errors as you move through the sound and word. Focus on feeling the feel of change or not overcorrecting your abnormalities as you read carefully.

Do it even if you feel self-conscious about your pause or the way you pronounce the dreaded word. Because there is no other option, this is where your perseverance will pay off. As you get better at dealing with your anticipated blocking in this new manner, you'll notice that the pause gets shorter and shorter.

It may seem tempting, but you must not under any circumstances use the break as a postponement. Use the pause to plan and practice your course of action.

This pre-block adjustment is a crucial component of your treatment plan. You are well on your way to speaking freely and effectively if you can proceed without any problems through an anticipated block. Pre-block corrections should be practiced on both feared and unfeared words—or the first word of a sentence—but not as a shortcut to begin a phrase. While learning the technique, some stutterers pre-blocked each word, but this is not necessary. A strong pre-block has lasting effects.

Determine how you often hesitate on a few words that you think you might block, then choose the alterations you need to make and implement them as soon as you reach the word. Pre-block whenever you sense problems and activate your controls. Maintain this practice until you can detect the necessary corrections for any form of block automatically. You should feel relieved knowing that your stuttering is under control as a result.

You can start gradually removing the delay once you have used pre-block fixes so frequently that they are second nature to you. When you sense difficulty coming up on a sound a few words ahead, you can get ready for what needs to be done when you say the feared word while saying the words in between.

Once you have time to determine how you will make the necessary modifications, shift your speech into low gear (slow down). Then, as you feel your way through the word, move gently and fluently. You can achieve this goal quite fast, but it would be preferable for you to first stop and take a break in order to give yourself the time you need to adequately prepare for any potential difficulties.

As you become more adept at pre-block adjustments, you will gain confidence in your capacity to restrain your voice and proceed through any block according to a pre-planned path. To form the sounds and utter the phrases smoothly, you plan the movements you must make and how you must do them. It's crucial to finish what you start. You stutter, and you should now know how to stop doing what you have been doing.

15

Dealing With Discouragement

If you stutter as many people do, you may occasionally feel very discouraged while you attempt to make progress with your speech. This can be the case because you are not recovering as rapidly as you believe you should or because you occasionally relapse and experience significant hardship.

The latter may happen if you are speaking more naturally when you encounter an embarrassing scenario, tense up, and perform poorly. You become very discouraged as a result, which damages any faith you may have had in your ability to move forward.

Stuttering, regrettably, appears to be especially prone to recurring. Additionally, it should be noted that several elements are working against your efforts and have a propensity to trigger relapses or regressions.

Relapses might happen as a result of natural inclinations to resume some of your previous behaviors, like avoidance or denial of your stuttering. You have started to experience some fluency, and to preserve that fluency, your natural impulses lead you to act in the manner to which you have been accustomed over a long period. You might start to stutter again in tiny imitations.

When old habits return, you shouldn't berate yourself. Nevertheless, you should be aware of these instances as warning signs to return to work and reevaluate your adherence to the guidelines. These minor sentiments of avoidance or any forcings will disappear as you deal with them.

The fact that practically every stutterer's intensity tends to change occasionally is one aspect that could lead to dissatisfaction. You speak more clearly than at other times of the day. Although this might be caused by several environmental factors, it appears that these variations might persist, making a breakdown more likely to occur.

Another potential downside of improvement is when your expectations get too high. This may have happened when you accepted a rule or guideline that caused you to improve so quickly that you were convinced it was the solution to your problem. Failure also tends to make the future look bleak if trust in that specific procedure is already low.

Truthfully, there are times when a single rule or corrective procedure can account for a sizable portion of the solution to your issue. However, applying the various methods typically ensures more consistent success.

Another factor that contributes to some stutterers' discouragement is their unrealistic expectations of perfection. Some people believe they should be able to speak without any hesitation or stumbles at all. Expecting perfection might put unnecessary strain on people. Your aim should be to speak easily and without exertion because even average speakers struggle with fluency.

Additionally, it is possible that your brain's speech-controlling region and the timing sequence of your speaking muscle movement are more naturally coordinated in you. Other folks are likewise like that.

But if your stuttering began when you were very young, there may be greater justification for this being the case in your case. You could have struggled harder than other kids did when learning to talk as a child. Additionally, the aforementioned absence of superior natural coordination may have played a role in the onset of your stuttering.

As you are aware, coordination is a physical quality that differs from person to person. Some kids walk earlier than others, and some kids pick up talking more quickly than others. A champion golfer, for instance, has excellent synchronization between the region of the brain that manages the movement and how it affects the movement of his golf clubs. In any event, striving for faultless speech is not realistic for people who stutter.

The majority of stutterers have periods of relative fluency accompanied by hope, followed by blocks accompanied by despondency. When you experience a relapse from fluency, try to discover how to pinpoint the cause. Check your compliance with the rules, and whenever you speak, avoid straining or stuttering excessively.

We would like to stress that there is no need to feel bad about stuttering; it does not indicate that you are a failure. The majority of stutterers occasionally lose hope. The adversary of stuttering must be repeatedly subdued since they are tenacious foes. Recognize this fact. Therapy may occasionally be a frustrating experience, but you might be able to view it as having the potential to show what could be done to improve speech.

The likelihood of relapse makes it challenging to achieve fluency fast. It requires time. Slow and gradual changes are the most effective strategy to eliminate stuttering for good.

Conclusion

Let's go through the scenario and discuss any advancements you may have made. Perhaps you've been reading this book purely to get knowledge about stuttering and how a therapy program functions. If so, we're glad you liked reading it. You ought to now be more familiar with the effects of this intricate issue as a result.

But if you stutter and have been attempting the suggested methods honestly, you should have discovered that you could alter your speaking mannerisms by allowing your speech to be guided by the guidelines established by the ground rules.

When you first started using this program, we assume you honestly explored the therapy technique where you spoke slowly, steadily, and for a long period, which has helped some stutterers. You should have been able to communicate more easily in these challenging situations if you had adopted this leisurely, drawing way of speaking. We understand that even if this way of speaking definitely helped you, you might not always want to speak in that manner.

You should have been able to tell if you have the requisite willpower to stick with therapeutic procedures that would help you fix your condition by experimenting with that method. We believe you made that decision.

The ground rules were allegedly worked on after that. Expecting total, satisfactory compliance with all their aims would be unreasonable. But if you followed these instructions, you probably discovered that you may limit your difficulties, in part by altering your attitudes and thoughts regarding your stuttering and, in part, by altering the abnormal behaviors connected to your stuttering behavior.

You've started with the rules. Some of them didn't demand that you cease stuttering; instead, they requested you make some calming adjustments to your speaking style. For example, you were first advised to develop the habit of speaking slowly and purposefully. Even more crucially, you were also instructed to stutter easily, subtly, and fluently while delaying the beginning sounds of your feared words and the transition to the following sounds. Additionally, it was advised that you try to change the volume and speed of your speech and talk melodiously while expressing yourself.

Do you now have a practice of speaking slowly and deliberately at all times? And do you deliberately stutter in a manner that is as expressive and musical as possible—easily, gently, and smoothly? You are speaking with less strain and the frequency and severity of your difficulties must have decreased if you complied with these suggestions. That indicates that you have advanced somewhat.

Then, to lessen your fear of difficulty, you were asked to change several practices that fed that anxiety. One guideline instructed you to stop attempting to hide the fact that you stammer and to instead publicly acknowledge it. Furthermore, you were to halt any avoidance, substitution, or postponement behaviors you had developed to get around anticipated problems. That one was also challenging. Similarly, you were instructed to consistently keep up natural eye contact when stuttering to lessen feelings of humiliation.

Have you truly improved your behavior and attitude to the point where you are willing to talk openly about your stuttering with anyone? Do you make good eye contact with your listener even when you're having trouble? And can it be expected that you no longer make an effort to prevent, delay, or replace? If you have followed these guidelines, a lot of the stress and anxiety that plagues stutterers and raises their tension has been eliminated. Simply having some of your concerns lessened should have improved your quality of life.

All of the aforementioned was particularly important in assisting you in reducing some of the tension and worries that were the primary factors generating or exacerbating your problems.

Rule 7 requires you to carefully examine your stuttering pattern as your next action. It was required to perfectly mimic what your speech systems did when you stumbled in order to do this. As a result, by listening to yourself speak, you could clearly see what you performed unnaturally or erratically with your lips, tongue, and jaw—muscles that are not necessary for producing speech.

You were instructed to change or remove these incorrect speech muscle motions by using block corrections after receiving this invaluable specific information about them. These important steps were difficult to follow but were designed to stop or change the articulatory mistakes you made when stuttering.

By replacing outdated patterns with new ones, they were created to assist you in guiding your speech muscle movements simply and smoothly into, through, and out of your blockages. These steps ought to have made it easier for you to change the erratic movements that made you stutter.

Theoretically, this stopped you from stuttering, but in practice, it should have at least made it easier for you to talk without using as many blocking techniques as you had in the past—habits that you now know can be broken. The other regulations that weren't covered above were a part of your program, so we assume they weren't forgotten. One of them pushed you to speak continuously, without repeating yourself or going backward, to maintain the progress of your voice.

Another one suggested that you focus more and consider your level of fluency. You've spent enough time dwelling on your stutter and worrying about it. And the more it should have aided you in gaining confidence if you have made a point of feeling the level of fluency you possess. Furthermore, it is assumed that you have attempted to speak as frequently as possible since if not, you would not have had the opportunities to practice your speech.

We hope you were able to achieve the outcomes described above by adhering to the twelve rules or guidelines. Did you give it enough time? Where are you right now?

You have finished this therapy program if you have tried your best to adhere to all of these rules. We are unsure of how proficient you have gotten; you may have made significant progress or not. This book merely outlines a strategy that will succeed. You are responsible for the outcomes.

By sticking with this program, you are hopefully continuing to break whatever avoidance patterns you may have had and are now more willing to confess that you stutter. Your anxiety should have been greatly reduced as a result, and you should also have gained more self-confidence and stress tolerance.

Additionally, if you've learned nothing else, you should know that you can alter your speaking style. You can learn to regulate your stuttering if you can change the pattern of it. You desire and require a sense of control that makes it effortless and comfortable for you to speak.

And if you have the fortitude to remain with this program, we'll bet you're happy you didn't change your mind. However, even for those who have advanced quickly, we suggest vigilance. Even though it may sound strange, you might need to get used to fluent communication.

Depending on how you react, you might need to keep an eye on your speech as it gains fluency. For instance, you might speak so quickly that you fail to notice any potential avoidances or conflicts. Additionally, because you are not accustomed to speaking openly, any inability to explain yourself through carefully chosen phrases or sentences may make you doubt your capacity to communicate.

Unfortunately, as it has been noted, stuttering appears to be particularly prone to recurring. You must be careful not to fall back into old routines. If you're not careful, habits that you developed years ago and have practiced for a long time may reappear. You could occasionally run into old fears.

The most crucial thing to keep in mind if you have these kinds of worries is that being willing to stammer in a modified style can greatly aid in maintaining and reinforcing your fluency. Do your utmost to ensure that your speech is guided by the norms to help prevent backsliding or regression. You can always communicate more effectively and less strenuously by using these common-sense strategies. Also, watch out for starting to avoid it.

Block repairs are always an option if you encounter any odd difficulties. In any case, it can be a good idea to occasionally study and rehearse them as you might always be able to use them effectively. You should continue to grow more assured in your capacity to restrain your words as time goes on. Be forceful since you will feel more free from fear the more confidence you have.

It will be beneficial if you assume a generally upbeat mindset. Remind yourself that you can and will get through your challenge. You will advance more quickly if you can develop an assertive mindset and pair it with regulated approaches. Be bold, have faith in your abilities, and believe in yourself.

On the other hand, try not to demand or expect too much. Avoid being overly eager to speak well too quickly and refrain from placing unreasonable demands on your speech. And don't fall for the fallacy that simply because you don't stutter, you are smart, charming, and persuasive by default.

Don't feel as though you need to provide evidence if someone claims you are cured. Instead, admit that you still stutter and demonstrate to them that you can do so by doing it on purpose. You won't feel any pressure to stop stuttering if you consistently refer to yourself as one. Keep in mind that most stuttering is caused by trying not to stutter.

Your speech doesn't need to be flawless, just like other people's. Whether they stammer or not, most people lack verbal fluency and imperfect speech. Stuttering is a tenacious handicap, and if you have overcome it to the point where you are fearless, you can no longer classify it as such. As challenging as life is, therapy is challenging. Believe in yourself.

We would also like to reiterate that there is no justification for you to live the rest of your life stuttering helplessly and being sad if you have only been reading this book for informational purposes.

You can succeed because others have. Set goals for success and believe that you can accomplish them.

Made in the USA
Las Vegas, NV
18 October 2024